Identified

Ephesians Bible Study for Youth

LaBreeska Ingles

Table of Contents

Letter to the reader 2

Acknowledgements 4

Week 1 - Chosen

Large Group Session - Introduction . 5
Why we study the Bible 8
Ephesians 1 - Day 1 11
Ephesians 1 - Day 2 16

Week 2 - Included

Large Group Session 22
Ephesians 2 - Day 1 25
Ephesians 2 - Day 2 30

Week 3 - Adopted

Large Group Session 36
Ephesians 3 - Day 1 40
Ephesians 3 - Day 2 45

Week 4 - Called

Large Group Session 51
Ephesians 4 - Day 1 54
Ephesians 4 - Day 2 60

Week 5 - Imitators

Large Group Session 67
Spiritual Gifts Survey 71
Ephesians 5 - Day 1 74
Ephesians 5 - Day 2 79

Week 6 - Equipped

Large Group Session 85
Ephesians 6 - Day 1 88
Ephesians 6 - Day 2 94

Week 7

Large Group Session - Finale 102

About the Author 105

A Letter to the Reader

I wrote this Bible Study for my church youth group. When I was a teenager, my youth pastor introduced me to engaging written Bible studies. I loved diving deep into the Bible with my workbook and pencil, and it shaped my life in many ways. I created this study of Ephesians when I became a parent of teenagers and the leader of our church youth group. We had so much fun exploring Ephesians together. Many of the youth said that they were challenged by the scriptures, and that they had an increased desire to study the Bible more.

Each week consists of:

- A youth group lesson plan
- Suggestions for small group breakouts
- Two take home studies for the student

All of these pieces complement each other, but you can also pick and choose what best fits the teens you are working with.

If you are buying this Bible Study for yourself (or your teen), you do not have to complete the large group lesson.

For the large group sessions with my youth group, I divided the 20 students into 4 or 5 small groups to provide time for discussing what they were learning. The small groups competed against each other in the large group games. Each large group lesson reviews what the students learned in the previous week and introduces the next week's chapter of Ephesians.

If you are a parent or a teacher, you could use this Bible study as Sunday school material, homeschool curriculum, or as a lesson plan for your home group gatherings. I pray that each of you are empowered by the word of God as we launch into this experience together. May God lead you and guide you as you study His Word.

- LaBreeska

Acknowledgements

I want to dedicate this book to the Peytonsville Church Youth Group in Thompson Station, Tennessee. I loved our time together! You changed my life forever, and I am forever grateful for each of you and your beautiful families.

I need to recognize my lovely editor, Kristen Ownby, who crossed all the t's and dotted all the i's. You're not only a great editor, but an awesome youth leader and friend.

I would like to give a special thanks to my family. My husband Brian is also the book's designer and my all time encourager. I would have just put my little binder of Bible study notes on a shelf if you hadn't pushed me to share it with the world.

And to my little loves, Judah, River, Noa, and Liam… thanks for sharing mommy with the church work and editing process. I pray that your love for Jesus and His words are what you build your entire life upon.

Chosen

Large Group Session

Introduction Week 1

Small Groups (10 minutes):

Divide the class into small groups. These will be your small groups for the next six weeks.

Pass out the Ephesians Bible study books if you haven't already. Walk through the book and discuss how the lessons are to be completed. Allow the students time to explore and ask questions. Assign the first week's lessons to be completed by the next large group meeting.

Ask the students how they feel about starting a weekly Bible study.

1. Are they nervous?
2. Are they reluctant to give up their free time to do more "homework?"
3. What are they hoping to get out of this commitment?

Large Group Game (30 minutes):

We want to leave the students with a memorable impression of how important the word of God is for their life.

Before the game, print the "Why We Study the Bible" scriptures from the end of this lesson. Tape each Bible verse to a movie-sized candy box. Hide the candy/verses around your property.

When the students gather for the large group game time, read the following scripture: "I have hidden Your word in my heart that I might not sin against You. How sweet are Your words to my taste, sweeter than honey to my mouth!" (Psalm 119:11 and 119:103). Talk about how candy is awesome, but the words of God are sweeter and have better, long-lasting benefits. Discuss how this is possible.

Bible Verse Scavenger Hunt: Release the students to hunt the candy treasures. Once they bring in the bounty, pour each candy in a separate bowl to create a candy buffet. The students can get a new bowl and scoop out their favorite candies into their bowl to create their own candy concoction.

Gather the students together and read through each of the scriptures attached to the candy boxes. Discuss each verse and what it says about the gift of the scriptures.

Closing (5 minutes):

Pray together that this Bible study will be life-changing for each person in the room.

Why We Study the Bible

2 Timothy 3:16-17

All Scripture is God-breathed and is useful for teaching, rebuking, correcting and training in righteousness, so that the servant of God may be thoroughly equipped for every good work.

Joshua 1:8

Keep this Book of the Law always on your lips; meditate on it day and night, so that you may be careful to do everything written in it. Then you will be prosperous and successful.

Psalm 119:105

Your word is a lamp for my feet, a light on my path.

Psalm 119:11 & 103

I have hidden Your word in my heart that I might not sin against You. How sweet are Your words to my taste, sweeter than honey to my mouth!

2 Timothy 2:15

Do your best to present yourself to God as one approved, a worker who does not need to be ashamed and who correctly handles the word of truth.

Deuteronomy 11:18-23

Fix these words of mine in your hearts and minds; tie them as symbols on your hands and bind them on your foreheads. Teach them to your children, talking about them when you sit at home and when you walk along the road, when you lie down and when you get up. Write them on the doorframes of your houses and on your gates, so that your days and the days of your children may be many in the land the Lord swore to give your ancestors, as many as the days that the heavens are above the earth. If you carefully observe all these commands I am giving you to follow—to love the Lord your God, to walk in obedience to Him and to hold fast to Him—then the Lord will drive out all these nations before you, and you will dispossess nations larger and stronger than you.

Acts 17:11

Now the Berean Jews were of more noble character than those in Thessalonica, for they received the message with great eagerness and examined the scriptures every day to see if what Paul said was true.

Hebrews 4:12

For the word of God is alive and active. Sharper than any double-edged sword, it penetrates even to dividing soul and spirit, joints and marrow; it judges the thoughts and attitudes of the heart.

Proverbs 2:1-5

My son, if you accept my words and store up my commands within you, turning your ear to wisdom and applying your heart to understanding—indeed, if you call out for insight and cry aloud for understanding, and if you look for it as for silver and search for it as for hidden treasure, then you will understand the fear of the Lord and find the knowledge of God.

Psalm 1:2

...but whose delight is in the law of the Lord, and who meditates on His law day and night.

Matthew 22:29

Jesus replied, "You are in error because you do not know the scriptures or the power of God."

Psalm 19:7-11

The law of the Lord is perfect, refreshing the soul. The statutes of the Lord are trustworthy, making wise the simple. The precepts of the Lord are right, giving joy to the heart. The commands of the Lord are radiant, giving light to the eyes. The fear of the Lord is pure, enduring forever. The decrees of the Lord are firm, and all of them are righteous. They are more precious than gold, than much pure gold; they are sweeter than honey, than honey from the honeycomb. By them your servant is warned; in keeping them there is great reward.

Romans 10:17

Consequently, faith comes from hearing the message, and the message is heard through the word about Christ.

Chosen

Ephesians 1

DAY 1

Ephesians was written by the Apostle Paul to the church in Ephesus. Paul was in a Roman prison when he wrote this letter. To understand the point of the letter, you must understand the culture of the city of Ephesus during that time.

Ephesus was a bustling capital of Asia. It was the home of the temple of Artemis, a Greek god of fertility and protection. Artemis wasn't the only false god worshiped in this city. It was very common for the people of Ephesus to worship many different false gods to get protection and wealth.

In fact, much of the city's economy depended on the Greek gods because tourists would travel from all over the Roman Empire to see the temple of Artemis. The Ephesians made money off of this idolatry.

What do you think it would be like to live in a city like this?

_____

_____

Write Exodus 20:3 below.

_____

_____

We do not worship little golden idols, but sometimes we put things before God and that is also idolatry. The definition of idolatry is "extreme admiration, love, or reverence for something or someone." Take a moment and ask the Holy Spirit if you admire or love anything or anyone more than God.

> *Holy Spirit,*
>
> *If there is anything that I treasure more than You, please reveal that to me. Is there anything that I would rather do than spend time with You? Is there something that I give my time and money to that You do not agree with?*

Write a list of things you have put before God below.

_____   _____

_____   _____

Take a moment and read Ephesians 1:1-14. After you have read it, go back through those fourteen verses and **underline** every adjective or descriptive phrase that Paul uses to describe the church. For example:

> "...to God's holy people in Ephesus, the faithful in Christ Jesus..." *Ephesians 1:1.*

Make a list of these underlined adjectives or descriptive phrases below.

_____   _____

_____   _____

_____   _____

_____   _____

Now, go back and **circle** the words or phrases from this list that you feel describe you.

Are there words or phrases from this list that you don't understand? Write the definitions of the words you do not understand below. (You can look up the definition in a dictionary or on the internet.)

_____

_____

One of the words I underlined in this scripture was "blameless." That word means "innocent of wrongdoing." Obviously, I am not blameless. I have done wrong things in my life. I have not always been innocent.

What does Ephesians 1:7 say about the sins in my life?

Look up the word "redemption." Write the definition below.

When we give our lives to Jesus, He exchanges His blood from the cross for our sins (or wrongdoings). He freely gives us a clean slate. Not only do we get complete forgiveness, but then we get to be His adopted sons and daughters, completely blameless and holy, just like Him (Ephesians 1:5).

How does that make you feel? Write a prayer to God below thanking Him for all of the underlined words in Ephesians 1:1-14 that now describe you.

Dear Jesus,

Chosen

Ephesians 1

DAY 2

Ephesians chapter 1 begins by Paul reminding the Ephesian church who they are in Christ Jesus. They are sons and daughters, chosen by God. They are forgiven, redeemed, and marked with purpose. The church needed to be reminded of who they were in Christ Jesus because they lived in a city full of false idol worship, greed, and blatant sin.

Paul ends this chapter with a prayer, thanking God for his Ephesian brothers and sisters. This prayer could be prayed over each of us. You could pray this prayer over your friends and families today. This prayer is a model, similar to how Jesus taught His disciples to pray.

Write the Lord's Prayer below. You may know it from memory, but if you don't, you can copy it from Matthew 6:9-13.

Depending on your translation, you may or may not have seen the following sentence at the end of the Lord's Prayer in Matthew 6:9-13:

> *"For Yours is the Kingdom and the power and the glory forever. Amen."*

This part of the prayer was included in the original Greek manuscripts but left out of some translations. People love to debate about whether this statement should be included in the Lord's Prayer, but I think we can all agree that God has the Kingdom, the power, and the glory forever, so:

1. **Add that to the written prayer you copied above.**

2. **Underline all of the words in the Lord's Prayer that describe God.**

3. **Circle the parts of the prayer that are asking God for something.**

4. **Take time to memorize this prayer if you haven't already.**

Look at Ephesians 1:19-23. In your Bible, **underline the descriptions of God listed in these scriptures.**

Verse 21 says Christ was raised "far above all rule and authority, power and dominion, and every name that is invoked..."

Write what that means below. How is it similar to the ending of the Lord's Prayer?

Ephesians 1:22-23 says the Church is Christ's body. Read 1 Corinthians 12:12-27 and what it says about the Church being the body of Christ.

What do these verses tell us about the church being a body?

How should we treat our friends, knowing that we are all a part of one body?

_____

_____

_____

Paul prayed for his friends in Ephesians 1:15-19. Just like you circled the things you were asking God for in the Lord's Prayer written above, **circle the things Paul asked God for concerning the church in Ephesians 1:15-19 (in your Bible).**

Choose a person from your youth group to pray for. **Write a prayer below that uses some of the same words that Paul used. Feel free to write it in your own words.** Use Paul's prayer as a model.

_____

_____

_____

_____

_____

Here is my prayer for each of you:

Holy Spirit,

I pray for each student trying to read and understand Your Scripture today. I pray that the eyes of their hearts may be enlightened. I pray that they would really know deep down the hope that they have in You. I ask that they would live like they own the riches of Your glorious inheritance. I pray You would fill them with Your great power and teach them to love each other and work together as one body. In Jesus' name, amen.

Small Groups (10 minutes):

Divide the class into assigned small groups.

The goal of today is to discuss how Week 1's Bible study went and to introduce Ephesians chapter 2 for next week. In each group, ask how the students felt about their Bible studies this week. Allow time for discussion.

1. Ask the students to point out what parts of the Bible study were difficult for them. (Maybe they didn't understand the question. Maybe they didn't understand one of the Bible passages.)
2. Ask the students what idols they repented of in their personal lives.
3. Ask them who they felt led to pray for in Week 1, Day 2's prayer.
4. Ask a student to read Ephesians 2:11-13 in preparation for today's games.

Large Group Game (30 minutes):

Introduce the game: "You just read a portion of the Bible about Gentiles versus Jews. We are going to play a game that involves an 'us versus them' mentality. As we play this game, keep in mind how it relates to our scripture verses."

Capture the Flag: Divide the students into two teams. Team A are the Gentiles. Team B are the Jews. Set boundaries and rules for the game. Each team has a flag and a given area with boundaries. They must hide their flag in plain sight on their side. The goal of the game is to try to keep your flag safe while also sending team members into "enemy" territory to steal the opposing flag. A team wins by stealing the opposing flag and bringing it back to their side.

You may tag members of the opposing team when they cross into your territory. The tagged individual will go into an imaginary jail to wait until a teammate from their side tags them out.

There are many variations of this game on the internet. Feel free to create the best experience for your space.

Questions to ask after the game:

1. What does this game have to do with the passage of Ephesians we read in our small group?
2. How does it feel to be on a team? Do you feel empowered, encouraged, held back, or prohibited?
3. How does it feel when you are on the wrong side? Do you feel nervous? Do you feel welcome?
4. What does Ephesians 2 say about doing life in teams or working against each other? Does God want us to be fighting each other or unifying together?

Closing (5 minutes):

Everyone knows how it feels to be included, and everyone knows how it feels to be left out. Ask someone to read Ephesians 2:19-22. What does this passage say about how we should work together?

Pray together about how we can be more like Jesus and work together to bring others closer to Him. Encourage all of the kids to complete their Bible studies for next week.

Included

Ephesians 2

DAY 1

Before we begin today, take a moment and ask the Holy Spirit to help you today. The Holy Spirit is the one who reveals the mystery of Scripture to us. He is a teacher and He knows how to highlight what you need for each moment.

> *Holy Spirit,*
>
> *I invite You to speak to me today through Ephesians. Reveal hidden mysteries to me. Teach me things I never knew. Highlight what is important for today. Lead me closer to Jesus. Amen.*

Read Ephesians 2:1-3. It describes what life before Christ is like.

Underline descriptions in your Bible of what it is like to live without Christ.

What is the definition of the word "transgression" (verse 1)?

_____

_____

What is the definition of the word "gratifying" (verse 3)?

_____

_____

When you were living in sin, who were you following (verse 2)?

Who is the "ruler of the kingdom of the air" (verse 2)?

Satan is described as the spirit who is working in those who are disobedient. Have you ever thought about how you are always following someone? We are either following God through the Holy Spirit or Satan through disobedience. There are two sides. One is death. One is life.

Whose side are you on?

Read Ephesians 2:4-10.

Underline the descriptions in your Bible listed for those who are following Christ.

Fill in the blank for verse 5.

"...made us _____ with Christ even when we were _____

in transgressions—it is by _____ you have been saved..." (NIV).

Verse 6 talks about us being raised up with Christ. We were dead, then resurrected in the Spirit. Think about baptism. **How is this resurrection demonstrated in the act of baptism? Write your answer below.**

Have you ever been baptized? ***Write about your baptism in your closing prayer today.*** *If you have never been baptized, pray about that decision and ask the Holy Spirit what He would have you do.*

What is the definition of the word "grace" (verse 5)?

In verses 8-9, circle the words that describe how you have been saved.

When we are following Jesus, we are living, walking miracles. We are resurrected from a dead life (living in sin) to a life filled with grace and kindness.

If you chose to follow Jesus at a young age, you may not have felt that dramatic shift of living in darkness, then being born again to walk in the light. God has protected you from so many years of painful separation.

Think about how dramatic Paul's conversion was. He was murdering Christians one day, then born again and teaching the Gospel of Jesus Christ another day. He would tell you that you have a lot to be thankful for.

Write a prayer to God, thanking Him for your new life (and your baptism).

_____

_____

_____

_____

_____

_____

Included

Ephesians 2

DAY 2

"Show me your ways, O Lord, teach me your paths; guide me in your truth and teach me, for you are God my Savior, and my hope is in you all day long." Psalm 25:4-5

Read Ephesians 2:11-22.

Ephesians 2:11 discusses circumcised versus uncircumcised. You may need to ask your parents what circumcision is in order to understand this commandment. Let's look at when the covenant of circumcision began in the Bible.

Read Genesis 17:10-14.

List what the rules of circumcision were below.

In New Testament writings, you will often hear a debate about Jews versus Gentiles.

Name someone you know who was a Jew?

There are many Jews you could have listed above. Jesus was a Jew. Most of the characters from the Old Testament were Jews. Jews had to follow the law of circumcision, and that act may have seemed harsh to other cultures. This is why the Jews were sometimes called "the circumcision" (verse 11).

Look up what a "Gentile" is on the internet. Write the answer below.

_____

_____

Who do you know that is a Gentile?

_____

You are most likely a Gentile, unless you were born into a Jewish family. Many of the people in Ephesus were Gentiles. Paul had a special calling to tell the Gentiles about Jesus, but he was a Jew. Paul had to teach the Jewish believers in Ephesus that the Gentiles were a part of God's family now, too.

Fill in the blank for Ephesians 2:13.

"But now in Christ Jesus you who once were _____ _____ have been

brought _____ by the _____ of Christ" (NIV).

Reread Ephesians 2:14-16.

How did Jesus break down the wall that separated the Jews and the Gentiles?

_____

_____

In the Old Testament, one of the ways Jews were separated from Gentiles was by circumcision (a procedure involving blood). In the New Testament, Jesus reunited the Gentiles into the family of God by the blood He shed on the cross.

Have you ever felt left out of a group? Describe how that felt below.

_____

_____

_____

Ephesians 2:19 says that we are now all members of God's

_____ . That means we are all in one family.

Jesus died on the cross so that, by His blood, we could become a part of His family. Verse 20 says that Jesus is the cornerstone of this large family (or building) that joins us into one temple where the Holy Spirit can dwell.

Ephesians 2:20-21 describes the Church as a building.

In your Bible, underline the descriptions of that building.

Write Ephesians 2:22 below.

_____

_____

_____

You may not deal with the competition between the Jew and the Gentile, but you know what it is like to be included in a group and excluded by a group. **How can you be like Jesus and include others into your group this week?**

_____

_____

_____

Jesus,

Help us to be people who welcome others into Your family with open arms. Show us people who feel left out or pushed aside. Please make us a dwelling place of Your Spirit that draws others to You. Amen.

Adopted

Large Group Session
Week 3

Small Groups (10 minutes):

In each group, ask the students how they felt about their Bible studies this week. Allow time for discussion.

1. Ask the students to point out what parts of the Bible study were difficult for them.
2. Ask the students to share about their personal salvation and baptism.

Large Group Clips & Game (30 minutes):

Today, we are going to watch two short videos about Paul.

Clips:

I like to show videos from The Bible Project called "The Apostle Paul" from Acts 8-12; then, there is one from Acts 13-21. You can watch both of these videos or choose videos of your own that overview the life of the Apostle Paul. Check out all of the great videos and resources from The Bible Project at the following url:

bibleproject.com

Now, look at your Bible study for Ephesians Chapter 3, Day 1. Complete this section together.

Read 2 Corinthians 11:23-28.

List below the sufferings and hardships that Paul lists in these verses.

_____   _____

_____   _____

_____   _____

_____   _____

_____   _____

Game:

This past week, in your Bible study, there was a question that said, "Have you ever thought about how you are always following someone?"

Follow the Leader Circle: We are going to play a follow-the-leader game where one person leaves the room. The other students sit in a circle and pick a leader to follow. When the person (who left the room) comes in, everyone is following the leader doing something like clapping their hands, snapping their fingers, or pretending to yawn. You must stay seated in your chairs.

Without being noticed, the leader changes their movement to something like touching their nose, tapping their toes, or playing with their hair. Everyone follows the leader without staring right at them. The motions keep changing until the person who first left the room guesses who the leader is.

<u>Questions to ask after the game:</u>

1. What does this game have to do with the thought that we are always following someone?
2. Have you ever noticed, in a group, that we sometimes start to behave like each other? Sometimes, we all want the same pair of shoes or want to cut our hair the same way. Why is that?
3. Who do we want to follow?
4. How do we know how to follow Jesus?

Closing (5 minutes):

Pray for each other. Take time to ask Jesus how we can be better followers. Encourage all of the kids to complete their Bible studies for next week.

Adopted

Ephesians 3
DAY 1

Mystery is defined as something that is difficult or impossible to understand or explain. Paul begins to reveal the secrets of a mystery in Ephesians chapter 3.

Take a moment and ask the Holy Spirit to reveal the mystery of this scripture to you as you study today.

Read Ephesians 3:1-6.

Underline the word "mystery" everytime it appears in this passage.

What is the mystery that Paul is referring to?

_____

Write Ephesians 3:6 below.

_____

_____

_____

_____

The big mystery that Paul is revealing is that the Gentiles are a part of the family of God. The Gentiles get to share this gift of Jesus with the Jews. This may not seem like a big secret to you, but to the Jews of Paul's day, this was a very controversial subject. Paul is teaching a brand new revelation.

Read Ephesians 3:7-13.

Underline every word or phrase that describes Paul in your Bible.

Paul was a Jewish teacher of the law. He was well known and respected in the temple. He was trained by a wise rabbi named Gamaliel. Paul was so zealous to uphold the Jewish law that he became obsessed with killing Christians.

Read Paul's own account of his previous life in Acts 22:1-21.

Underline what we know about Paul through these verses in your Bible.

Paul was enemy number one of the Church one day, then he became one of the most well-known church leaders in history. When he refers to his sufferings in Ephesians 3:13, he is talking about all of the hardships and persecutions that he faced after choosing to believe Jesus and follow Him.

Read 2 Corinthians 11:23-28.

List below the sufferings and hardships that Paul lists in these verses.

_____   _____

_____   _____

_____   _____

_____   _____

_____   _____

Would you be willing to endure all of these things listed above for Jesus? We would like to believe we would, but most of us haven't experienced real persecution in our lifetime.

Write a prayer asking God to give you the strength to endure hard things for His Kingdom.

Write your prayer below.

_____

_____

_____

_____

Adopted

Ephesians 3
DAY 2

Read Ephesians 3:14-21 out loud as your opening prayer today.

This passage was a prayer that Paul prayed over the church of Ephesus. It is a beautiful prayer so rich and full of who God is and how He lives in us and through us. Let's explore it together.

Fill in the blank for Ephesians 3:14-15.

"For this reason I kneel before the _____, from whom

every _____ in heaven and on earth derives its name" (NIV).

> *God is the Father of families. God designed families. God wants us to live in families.*

Fill in the blank for Psalm 68:6.

"God sets the _____ in _____"
(NIV).

Maybe you have had a hard time in your family. Maybe your parents are divorced. Maybe you are a foster kid, bouncing from one home to another. **How is God putting every person in a family when people keep making mistakes and families keep breaking up?**

If your answer had something to do with the Church, then you are correct. Remember Ephesians chapter 2, where God is making us into one body or one building?

Write Ephesians 2:19 below.

Fill in the blank for Ephesians 3:16-17.

"I pray that out of His _____   _____ He

may strengthen you with _____ through His

_____ in your inner being, so that Christ may

_____ in your hearts through _____ "

(NIV).

Whom could you pray this prayer over? Who would you like to pray would receive power and love today? Write that person's name and today's date in your Bible. I like to write down whom I am praying for and when in my Bible, so that I can look back years from now and see how God answered my prayers.

Ephesians 3:17-19 says that being rooted and established in love gives us power together to grasp the love of God.

How can you be rooted and established in love?

_____

_____

How does Ephesians 3:18-19 describe God's love?

_____   _____

_____   _____

_____   _____

Verse 20 says that God is able to do immeasurably more than all we ask or imagine. I think we believe that, but sometimes it's hard to believe, right? But notice that verse 20 also says how God wants to do more than all we ask or imagine.

Write the end of Ephesians 3:20, starting after the words "ask or imagine."

_____

_____

It says "according to His power that is at work within us." God wants to work His miracles in and through us. We may think we are waiting on God to answer a prayer, but the truth may be that He is waiting on us to be His hands and feet.

Ask the Holy Spirit to show you any way you can be His hands and feet to show love to someone today. Write what He reveals to you below.

_____

_____

_____

Called

Large Group Session

Week 4

Small Groups (10 minutes):

In each group, ask how the students felt about their Bible studies this week. Allow time for discussion.

1. Ask the students to share about their families. Discuss how amazing families can be, but also discuss how it can be hard to get along in a family sometimes.
2. How can we improve our connection with our families?

Large Group Game (30 minutes):

Mafia Game: There are several different ways to play this game. Feel free to choose your favorite version. We get our students into a circle and have them close their eyes. Tap one student one time to signal they are the "mafia," tap a second student two times to signal they are the "detective," and tap a third student three times to signal they are the "doctor." The rest of the students are the townspeople.

Say, "Mafia awake," and that one student points to another student to "take out" and then closes their eyes. Next, say, "Doctor awake." That student can point to one student who they want to save, then they must close their eyes.

Now, everyone opens their eyes, and you announce what person was "taken out" by the mafia and who the doctor "saved." The detective can scan the crowd to see who looks guilty or who they suspect of being the "mafia." The detective can ask the townspeople their opinions, but the detective only gets one final guess at who the mafia is.

Announce whether the mafia was caught or not. Play this game as many times as you have time.

Questions to ask after the game:

1. How does this relate to Ephesians?
2. How is this game like our spiritual life? Who would be "out to get" us? What character in this game would be Jesus?
3. How can families support each other in life when someone is always out to get us, we make mistakes, or you don't always know who to trust, etc?
4. How is church like family?

Closing (10 minutes):

Pray together and ask God to help us to see each other as team members/family. Pray for clear eyes to see what the enemy is doing and how to overcome.

Look at Week 4, Day 1, second page. Have someone read Ephesians 4:7-13. Have everyone write the jobs/gifts that God gave the people in the Church in verse 11 in their Bible study folder.

List the jobs/gifts that God gave people in the Church in verse 11.

Called

Ephesians 4

DAY 1

Holy Spirit,

Please help me to know my calling and apply Your truth to my life so that I can be patient, gentle, and humble and live a life worthy of the calling I have received. Amen.

Underline the words in Ephesians 4:2 that describe how we should behave.

Read 1 Corinthians 13:4-5.

How are Ephesians 4:2 and 1 Corinthians 13:4-5 similar?

_____

_____

_____

Ephesians 4:1 says, "I urge you to live a life worthy of the calling you have received."

What is your calling?

_____

There is a lot of pressure on teenagers to "find their calling." Maybe this is because teenagers begin to prepare for college. And in college, you have to choose a major, and that major needs to reflect the job you plan to have to feed you and your future family for the rest of your life. Whew! That is a lot of pressure.

But take a deep breath, friend, because there is evidence that verse 2 is the "calling" referred to in verse 1.

Write Ephesians 4:2 on the lines provided.

_____

_____

_____

Your calling is to love. Love like Jesus loved. Love like 1 Corinthians 13:4-5 says to love. Whether you choose to go to Yale University or your local community college, love people. Whether you become a doctor or a janitor, love people. This is your high calling.

Read Ephesians 4:3-6.

Circle the word "one" every time you see it.

Make every effort to keep the unity of the Spirit. We are all one in Christ. Each of us are different people with different jobs, but we make up one gigantic body of Christ together.

Read Ephesians 4:7-13.

List the jobs/gifts that God gave people in the Church in verse 11.

_____   _____

_____   _____

_____   _____

Why did God give people these jobs/gifts in the Church? (Hint: look at verse 12.)

_____

_____

In order to know our role in the body of Christ, we need to explore the spiritual gifts that God has given us. We are all different. We don't need to try to copy someone else. We don't need to be jealous of someone else's gift. God has given you a special makeup to be a part of the body of Christ that no one else can be.

Read Ephesians 4:14-16.

How does verse 16 describe how you are important to the body of Christ?

_____

_____

Verse 14 says to stop being a baby. Well, not exactly, but it does say that when we go back and forth in listening to crafty people who teach things that are against God's word, then we are like infants.

How can we become mature in Christ?

_____

Fill in the blank below for Ephesians 4:15.

"Instead, speaking the _____ in love, we will grow to become in every

respect the _____ _____ of him who is the head, that is, Christ"

(NIV).

Write a prayer below. Ask God to show you how He has created you to fit into the body of Christ. Ask God to help you live a life worthy of the calling you have received.

Called

Ephesians 4

DAY 2

Holy Spirit,

"Hide your face from my sins and blot out all of my iniquity. Create in me a pure heart, O God, and renew a steadfast spirit within me. Do not cast me from your presence or take your Holy Spirit from me. Restore to me the joy of your salvation and grant me a willing spirit, to sustain me." Psalm 51:9-12

Read Ephesians 4:17-19.

Underline the words that describe the Gentiles in your Bible.

Paul is describing the lost Gentiles who are not following Jesus. He says they are futile in their thinking. They are darkened in their understanding. They are separated from the life of God and that has made them ignorant and caused them to harden their hearts.

Fill in the blanks for Ephesians 4:19.

"Having lost all _____, they have given themselves over to

_____ so as to indulge in every kind of _____..."
(NIV).

Have you ever gotten used to something uncomfortable? Maybe you didn't like a new shirt because the tags were scratching your neck, but after you wore it for a while, you stopped noticing. This is a physical act of losing sensitivity. Paul warns us about losing sensitivity to the Holy Spirit because it leads us into sensuality, impurity, and greed.

If you don't know the meaning of one of those words, ask your parents or look up the definition. I think we can all agree that we don't want to lose our sensitivity to the Holy Spirit.

Write a prayer below asking the Holy Spirit to make you sensitive. Ask Him to reveal anything that you have gotten used to that does not match Jesus.

_____

_____

_____

Read Ephesians 4:20-24.

One of the ways that we learn how to live like Christ is through teaching.

There are three steps that Paul says they were taught in verses 22-24.

List those three steps below.

1. _____

2. _____

3. _____

Paul said,

1. Put off the old corrupt self.
2. Be made new in your minds.
3. Put on the new self created to be like God.

Read Ephesians 4:25-28.

What does verse 25 say we should do?

_____

_____

Why is it so easy to lie to people? We've all done it. Have you ever told a little "white lie"? Someone asked you to come to their event, but you told them that you were busy instead of just admitting you didn't want to go. That's a lie. Your mom asked you if you finished your homework, and you told her you were almost done, even though you hadn't even started. Lie.

What emotion does Ephesians 4:26 warn us against?

_____

Is it a sin to be angry? No, but verse 26 says "in your anger," don't sin. **How can your anger lead to sin?**

_____

_____

What sin is described in Ephesians 4:28?

_____

What does verse 28 say you should do instead of stealing?

_____

_____

Read Ephesians 4:29-32.

Underline all of the instructions you find in verses 29-32.

Let's make a chart. Under Unwholesome Talk, make a list of things you have said that could be considered unwholesome. This may include bad words, inappropriate joking, complaining, etc. Under Building Others Up, make a list of compliments or encouragement you have given or could give to others.

Unwholesome Talk	**Building Others Up**
_____	_____
_____	_____
_____	_____

List the things that Paul says we need to get rid of in Ephesians 4:31.

_____	_____
_____	_____
_____	_____

Fill in the blank for Ephesians 4:32.

"Be _____ and compassionate to one another, _____

each other, just as in Christ _____ forgave You" (NIV).

Is there anyone that you need to forgive? It is important that we learn to forgive as Christ forgave us. That can be very hard. Do you need to forgive a bully? Do you need to forgive a friend who let you down? Do you need to forgive a parent who spoke harshly to you?

Take some time and write a prayer asking God to help you forgive freely.

_____

_____

_____

_____

Large Group Session

Week 5

Imitators

Small Groups (20 minutes):

In each group, ask how the students felt about their Bible studies this week. Allow time for discussion.

Take a few minutes to help each student answer the simple Spiritual Gifts Survey from Romans 12 (located at the end of this lesson). Discuss their top spiritual gifts during the small group time.

I wrote this particular Spiritual Gifts Survey (based on Romans 12) to be a quick and easy introduction to spiritual gifts, but you can find many different versions of Spiritual Gifts Surveys for youth on the internet. There are some options that are more extensive and may provide more conclusive results. Feel free to choose whatever works best for your group and the amount of time you have together.

Large Group Game (30 minutes):

Each one of us has different gifts, personalities, education levels, etc. God gave each of us spiritual gifts, and when we work together as one, we become ONE body of Christ.

Laundry Basketball Game: We are going to play a laundry basketball game where everyone has to sit in chairs. Set up two laundry baskets on opposite sides of the room to be the "goals." Choose a softer ball to be the basketball. The students must strategically decide where to place their chairs before the game begins. They may call time-out and redesign the chairs as they see new strategies (but only after one team has scored). They cannot stand up or remove their bottoms from their chairs.

After the game, discuss how each part of the team was important. You can't just depend on one part of the team to win the entire game. You have to have defense. You have to have offense. One man can't guard an entire team. The body of Christ is like that. It's important to know our spiritual gifts so that we know how to play well together as a team.

Questions to ask after the game:

1. How does your spiritual gift help others?
2. What spiritual gift was lowest on your scores? Who in the room has that gift as their highest?
3. How can we help each other in life by knowing how we are gifted?

Closing (10 minutes):

Pray together for spiritual eyes to see how the Lord has gifted us in the body of Christ. Ask God to help you see who is around you and what they carry.

Go to Week 5, Day 2, last two pages. Read Ephesians 5:22-33. Write out the lists of how the Church is like a wife and Christ is like the husband. Discuss how these help us to connect with God and each other.

Using Ephesians 5:22-33, list the behaviors that Christ/Husband should do on one side and what the Wife/Church should do in response on the other side.

<table>
<tr><th>Christ/Husband</th><th>Church/Wife</th></tr>
<tr><td></td><td></td></tr>
</table>

SPIRITUAL GIFTS SURVEY

Choose one of the following responses and place the number next to the statement. Then add up the four questions in each section and put the total next to the spiritual gift. After you have finished the test, circle the top scores to find your spiritual gift.

(1) Not me   (2) Rarely like me   (3) Sometimes like me   (4) Usually like me
(5) That's ME everytime!

Prophecy—able to hear God and deliver a message to others.

_____ I have dreamed things that have come true.

_____ I am open and honest with others.

_____ I recognize God speaking to me in different ways.

_____ Sometimes I see visions from God when I am praying for a person.

Total=_____

Serving—loves to support a cause through helping others.

_____ I love to work with my hands and help others out.

_____ I love to help others, even with things like dishes or mowing.

_____ I like to keep my room clean and organized.

_____ It's hard for me to say no when people ask for my help.

Total=_____

Teaching—desires to learn and teach others what they have learned.

_____ I love to learn new facts and study different themes on my own.

_____ I love to teach people about things they may have never heard about.

_____ It's easy for me to speak and express my thoughts clearly.

_____ I love explaining the whole story to people.

Total =_____

_____

Encouraging—one who encourages and guides others toward the right path.

_____ People say I am a very happy person and I love to talk.

_____ I like to tell people "good job."

_____ I have a very positive outlook on life.

_____ I notice what people can do well and I tell them.

Total=_____

_____

Giving—you save and create in order to give to those who are in need.

_____ Giving money or things to others makes me feel very happy.

_____ I like to create interesting gifts to give to people.

_____ I like to plan ways to give to people in need.

_____ I am good at making money, and I don't mind giving it away.

Total=_____

Leadership—you are able to see a goal and direct others toward that goal.

_____ I get a lot of joy from accomplishing a task.

_____ I always want to be the best at everything I do.

_____ I enjoy telling others what to do.

_____ I love leading and organizing when I'm in a group.

Total=_____

Mercy—one who feels the compassionate heart of God toward others.

_____ I get super sad when bad things happen to people.

_____ I look for the good in people and ignore the bad parts about a person.

_____ I enjoy peace and try to avoid conflict.

_____ I love helping people know how to solve their problems.

Total=_____

In which gift did you score highest? _____

Which was the lowest? _____

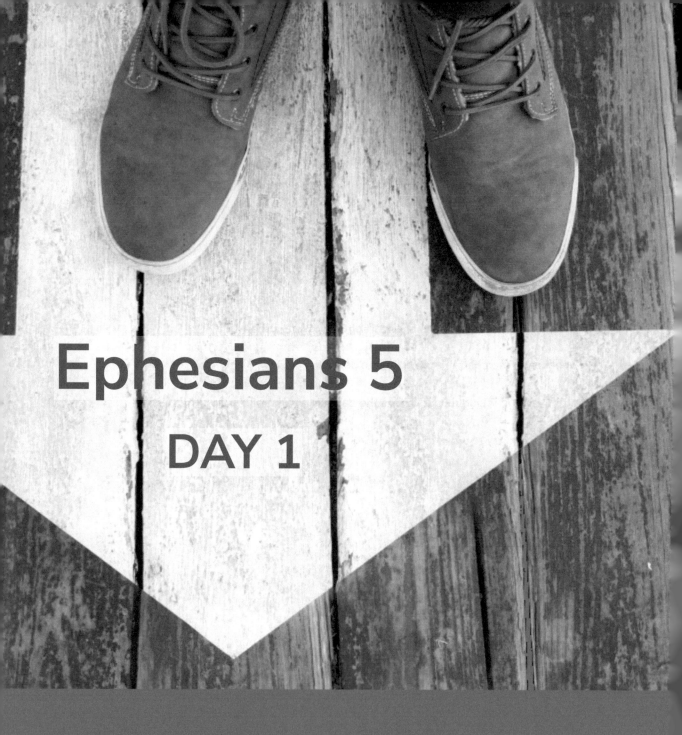

Ephesians 5

DAY 1

Imitators

Identity is who you are. Part of who you are is *whose* you are. If you are God's dearly loved children, then you should be imitators of God. You should look like God. You should behave like Jesus.

Read Ephesians 5:1-2.

If you are to live a life of love as Christ loved us, what does Christ's love look like?

_____

_____

Read Ephesians 5:3-6.

In your Bible, underline the words that are used to describe behaviors that are not like God.

This passage suggests that things like impurity, greed, and foolish talk are forms of idolatry. Remember in week one, when we prayed and asked God to reveal any idols we have? If you struggle with something on this list in Ephesians 5:3-6, verse 3 says these behaviors are improper for God's people. Verse 4 says that these negative behaviors are "out of place."

Is there a behavior that is "out of place" in your life? Is there something that does not imitate God?

_____

_____

Read Ephesians 5:7-14.

Verse 7 says that we should not partner with those who are walking in disobedience to God. Don't be deceived with empty words. Is there someone you are spending time with that is in disobedience with God?

Write Ephesians 5:8 below.

_____

_____

According to verse 9, what are the fruits of light?

_____   _____

_____

Fill in the blank for Ephesians 5:11-13 below.

"Have nothing to do with the _____ deeds of darkness, but

rather _____ them. It is _____ even

to mention what the disobedient do in _____ . But everything

_____ by the light becomes _____ ..."
(NIV).

These verses lead us to believe that sin likes to hide. When we are doing something that we know is wrong, we typically try to hide that sin, don't we? If you stole a cookie from the cookie jar as a child, you probably tried to do it when your mom wasn't watching. You may have snuck in the kitchen, kept as quiet as you could, then carried your stolen goods away to a hidden spot, so that you wouldn't be found. The very act of hiding may be an indicator that you feel guilty because you know what you are doing is wrong and you don't want to be found out.

Do you have anything that you are hiding? Is there anything you need to confess?

_____

_____

Write 1 John 1:9 below.

_____

_____

Re-read Ephesians 5:10 and 5:17.

What do these verses tell us to do?

_____

_____

We are IDENTIFIED as dearly loved children of God. Therefore, we want to find out what pleases the Lord and do it. We want to understand the Lord's will and do it. We want to be imitators of God. This is our identity.

We all mess up. We all have foolish moments or make bad decisions. We must seek to expose these mess-ups so that we do not become like the people who walk in darkness, because that is not who we are. That is not our identity.

Write a prayer to Jesus. Ask Him to help you confess your sins. Ask Him for the strength to expose your sins by confessing them to a trusted adult.

_____

_____

_____

_____

_____

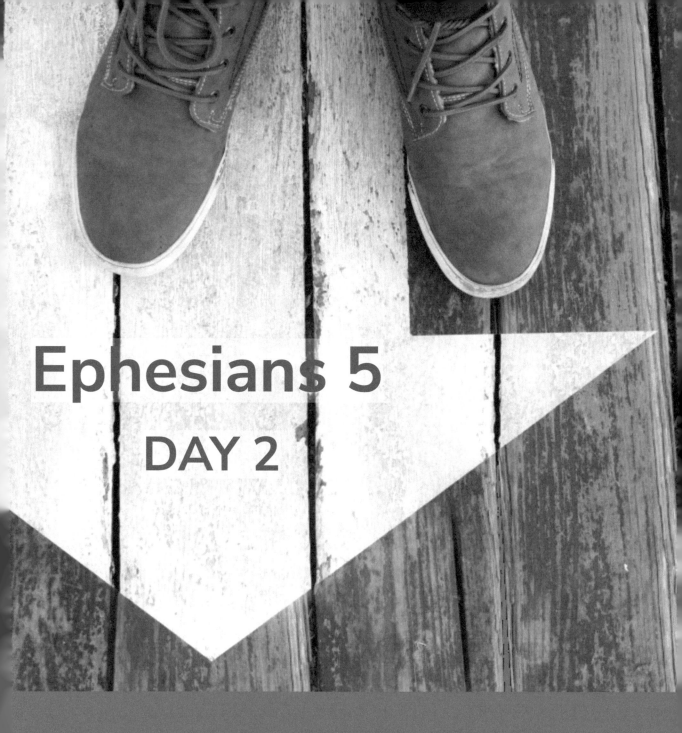

Ephesians 5

DAY 2

Imitators

Jesus,

I want to be an imitator of God. I ask that you wake me up and shine your light on these Scriptures. Help me to understand and align my life with your Word.   Amen

Read Ephesians 5:17-21.

Underline the things that these verses tell us we should do.

List them below.

_____   _____

_____   _____

_____   _____

These actions are acts of worship. When we sing songs to God, we are worshiping, but did you know that when you thank God for something, you are worshiping? Did you know that when you are submitting to each other, that is an act of worship also?

What is the one thing that these verses tell us we should not do?

_____

What does getting drunk with wine lead to (verse 18)?

_____

Write the definition of "debauchery" below.

_____

_____

Ephesians 5:18 says "do not get drunk on wine...instead, be filled with the spirit." Read Acts 2:4 and Acts 4:31.

What do these verses say about being filled with the Spirit of God?

_____

There are many different denominations that have different opinions about what it means to be filled with the Holy Spirit. Some people believe that you will always speak in tongues when you are filled with the Spirit. Some people believe you are filled with the Spirit when you are saved and baptized, and it doesn't matter if you speak in tongues. No matter what theology you believe, would you be willing to just repeat this prayer and invite the Holy Spirit to fill you completely and do what He wants in your life?

> *Holy Spirit,*
>
> *I ask that You come and fill me completely with Your Presence. I give You control of my mind, my spirit, and my body. I trust You. Have Your way in me. Amen.*

Read Ephesians 5:22-33.

These verses talk about how husbands and wives should behave toward each other. You probably aren't even thinking about marriage yet, so you don't need to be concerned with how to treat a spouse. However, let's look at these verses as how Christ and the Church treat each other.

Using Ephesians 5:22-33, list the behaviors that Christ/Husband should do on one side and what the Wife/Church should do in response on the other side.

<table>
<tr><td align="center"><u>**Christ/Husband**</u></td><td align="center"><u>**Church/Wife**</u></td></tr>
</table>

We want to love Jesus like a wife should love her husband. He already loves us the way that Ephesians 5 says a husband should love a wife. It is easy to respond to a love that is so deep and so tangible.

I invite you to respond to God's love toward you by writing a simple prayer of committing yourself to love God with everything you have.

_____

_____

_____

_____

Equipped

Large Group Session
Week 6

Small Groups (10 minutes):

In each group, ask how the students felt about their Bible studies this week. Allow time for discussion.

1. How did Ephesians chapter 5 tell us we should live?
2. What kinds of things should we be doing?
3. What kinds of things should we stop doing?

Large Group Clips & Game (30 minutes):

You could choose a movie clip to introduce teamwork to your group. I used a clip where Voltron unites from several different pieces into one stronger body. You could choose a sports movie where the team is working together to win the game. The video should suggest how the body of Christ could come together to be stronger together. You can choose different video clips to display these same ideas.

<u>Ask</u>: How does this video teach us that working together makes us stronger? How can we apply this to real life?

<u>Blob Tag Game</u>: This game of tag starts with one person who is "it." As the "it" person tags someone, they have to hold hands and run around to tag someone else. Each time the hand-holding chain of "it" people tags someone, they get added to the "blob." The person on each end of the blob has the power to tag someone. At the end of the game, the entire large blob is trying to capture the last person who has avoided capture thus far.

<u>Questions to ask after the game:</u>

1. What does this game have to do with Ephesians?
2. If the Church was the blob, how did they capture the lost people?
3. How can the Church (in real life) work together to bring people into the family of God?

Closing (5 minutes): Pray together. Ask God to make you look more like Him. Pray for your friends around you. Ask God to show you how you fit together as a team to be stronger.

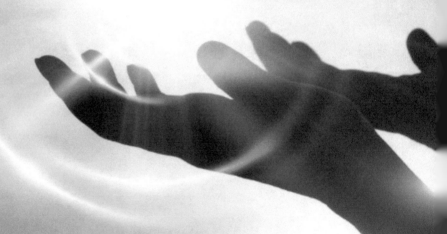

Equipped

Ephesians 6

DAY 1

Read Ephesians 6:1-9.

Ephesians chapter 6 begins with instructions for equipping leaders and followers. The way we follow someone determines whether or not we are ready for leadership. A good leader must first learn to be a humble servant. The first set of leaders and followers can be found in a family.

Write Ephesians 6:1 below.

_____

_____

Describe a time when you found it difficult to obey your parents.

_____

_____

What is the definition of the word "honor?"

_____

_____

Fill in the blank from Deuteronomy 5:16 below.

"_____ your father and your mother, as the Lord your God has

commanded you, so that you may live _____ and that it may go

_____ with you in the land the Lord your God is giving you" (NIV).

What are the two promises God gives you if you honor your parents?

_____   _____

> *Even when it is hard to obey, you are not just giving honor and respect to your parents, but you are securing your future. God will bless you when you honor your parents, especially when it is hard.*

What does Ephesians 6:4 warn fathers about?

_____

What is the definition of the word "exasperate?"

_____

_____

Have you ever felt exasperated by your parents? Describe below.

Have you ever disobeyed your parents? Did the disobedience lead to something good or bad? Describe below.

I've been a kid with parents, and I've been a parent with kids. I understand the importance of both of these commandments in Ephesians 6. None of us are perfect. We all make mistakes. I disobeyed my parents more than once. I have exasperated my kids. It happens. In a family, we must learn to forgive each other, serve one another, and try to do what is right.

Who is Paul addressing in Ephesians 6:5-9?

Slavery was a part of the culture that the Ephesians were living in during the time that Paul wrote this letter. Slavery in Ephesus often occurred when one people group was conquered by another. I 100% believe that slavery is wrong, but Paul was encouraging people in a different culture than I live in today. Let's examine these verses with that in mind.

In Ephesians 6:5, what did Paul tell the slaves to do?

_____

_____

In Ephesians 6:9, what did Paul tell the masters to do?

_____

_____

Now, let's apply this principle to our lives in our culture. Let's say that you got a job mowing your neighbor's yard. **How can you apply Ephesians 6:6-7 to your life?**

_____

_____

Holy Spirit,

I want to serve You by serving others. Help me to be an honest worker. Help me to honor my mom and dad, even when they mess up or yell at me. I know that you are using the leaders around me to equip me to be the kind of leader that you want me to be.

Amen.

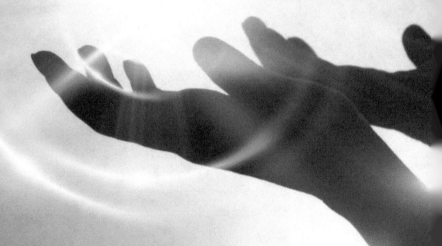

Equipped

Ephesians 6

DAY 2

Ephesians 6:10-24 is a famous passage of scripture about the armor of God. Today, we are going to learn how to be equipped in the Spirit in order to go to war against the devil and his schemes. Buckle up! Here we go!

Look up the word "equipped." Write the definition below.

Read Ephesians 6:10-24.

Ephesians 6:12 says our struggle is not against "flesh and blood," but against whom?

When Paul says we are not fighting against "flesh and blood," he means people. Have you ever had a disagreement with someone, and it felt like you could never forgive them for something they said or did? Paul is suggesting that you were never really fighting that person, but the devil and spiritual forces of evil. The devil is tricky.

In Ephesians 6:14-17, underline the pieces of the armor of God that are listed.

We are going to walk through this one step at a time. Draw a stick figure of a person below. As we introduce each layer of the armor, draw it on your stick figure.

1. **The Belt of Truth** (Draw a belt around your stick figure.)

Read John 14:6. **Who is truth?** _____ .

How do we buckle Jesus around us like a belt? This is a metaphor. We can put Jesus around us by giving our lives to Jesus and asking Him to fill us completely. When we put Jesus "on," we are putting on "truth."

2. **The Breastplate of Righteousness** (Draw a breastplate around your stick figure.)

> "If you know that He (Jesus) is righteous, you know that everyone who does what is right has been born of Him" (1 John 2:29).

A breastplate protects a warrior from arrows being shot at him by the enemy. Think of this: if you are wearing righteousness as a breastplate, that means that you are doing what is right in God's eyes and that righteousness protects your heart from the arrows of the devil.

What could those arrows look like in real life?

_____

_____

They could be arrows of temptation. Maybe the enemy is throwing arrows of self-doubt. Whatever the arrow, the breastplate of righteousness is protecting your heart and your life.

3. **Feet Fitted with Readiness from the Gospel of Peace** (Draw a pair of shoes around your stick figure.)

Fill in the blank with the second half of Romans 10:15.

"How _____ are the _____ of those who bring

good news" (NIV)!

We must always be equipped to share the truth of Jesus Christ with those around us. The true story of Jesus Christ brings peace to everyone who hears it. Being fitted with the readiness from the gospel of peace protects us from the enemy because it keeps us in the offensive position. We are on the move, doing the work of God, not laying around waiting for temptation and distraction from the enemy.

4. **Shield of Faith** (Draw a shield next to your stick figure.)

Fill in the blank for Romans 10:17.

"Consequently, _____ comes from hearing the message, and

the message is heard through the _____ of Christ" (NIV).

The shield of faith protects us from the flaming arrows of the evil one. What are the flaming arrows? Lies. Tricks. Deception. Temptation. Just like the breastplate of righteousness, this shield of faith is our defense. Having faith in Jesus and His Word protects us from all of the lies that are coming at us each day.

What kind of lies have you heard recently?

_____

_____

How can your faith in Jesus and His Word extinguish these lies?

_____

_____

5. **Helmet of Salvation** (Draw a helmet around your stick figure.)

> *"Salvation is found in no one else, for there is no other name under heaven given to mankind by which we must be saved"* Acts 4:12.

The helmet of salvation protects our minds. Salvation keeps us from confusion. It helps us to think straight, to make decisions, and to learn.

What is the definition of "salvation?"

_____

_____

6. **Sword of the Spirit/Word of God** (Draw a sword next to your stick figure.)

> *"For the word of God is alive and active. Sharper than any double-edged sword, it penetrates even to dividing soul and spirit, joints and marrow; it judges the thoughts and attitudes of the heart" Hebrews 4:12.*

The Word of God (Bible) is the sword of the Spirit. It is important to memorize Bible verses and declare them out loud when the enemy comes at you. These words of God will stab the enemy and make him run away like a scared puppy.

The Word of God also protects us by applying it to our lives. Hebrews 4:12 (above) says that the word of God discerns the thoughts and intentions of the heart. That means that the word of God can help us know what we need to change in our lives. Living a life devoted to God according to His word is the offensive position against the enemy.

Write a prayer below. Ask God to equip you with each piece of this spiritual armor to protect you and prepare you for spiritual warfare.

_____

_____

"Put on the full armor of God, so that when the day of evil comes, you may be able to stand your ground, and after you have done everything, to stand. Stand firm then!" Ephesians 6:13-14.

Large Group Session

Week 7 Finale

Small Groups (10 minutes):

In each group, ask how the students felt about their Bible studies this week. Allow time for discussion.

1. Discuss families.
2. Ask, "When is it hard to honor your parents?" Describe a time where you chose to honor your parents even though it was hard.

Large Group Game (30 minutes):

Armor Tag: Before class, print and cut out pictures of armor and put tape on each cut-out. There are several sites that have free printouts of the armor of God.

Put the taped pieces of armor on a table in the middle of the room. Have the students each grab one piece of armor and then yell, "Go!" to begin the game of tag. In this game of tag, the students are trying to tag someone else with the armor. After you've tagged one person, you may go back to the table and get another piece of armor to tag someone else.

Now that all of the armor is attached to people, randomly divide the students into teams (the number of teams is up to you). For the next 5 minutes, the students can try to steal armor from other teams and put it on their own self or their teammate.

At the end of the 5 minutes, have the students get together and count up how many pieces of armor they have. They must have one of every piece of the armor of God to win. If more than one team has all of the armor, then the winners are decided by who has the most complete armor sets.

<u>Questions to ask after the game:</u>

1. Why do we need to be equipped with all of the pieces of the armor of God?
2. What happens if you are missing one of the pieces of armor?

Closing (5 minutes):

Pray for each other to have the full armor of God. Ask the Holy Spirit to show you if there is any armor that you do not have.

Pray a blessing over each student and their families as we finish this Bible study together. May the words of God fill our minds and change our lives.

About the Author

LaBreeska Ingles is a wife, homeschool mom, and a lover of gardening. She has served in youth and children's ministries for over 25 years. She has a Master of Theology degree from Campbellsville University. She has been a social worker and teacher to children and teenagers, as well as a missionary volunteer in many countries. She currently writes Church Curriculum for children and youth at www.kidsministryteam.com, including:

- Encountering Jesus
- Experiencing the Holy Spirit
- Embracing the Father
- Kids Ministry School Training
- Kids Leading Kids

For more information or to reach out, email at contact@kidsministryteam.com.

Made in United States
Cleveland, OH
22 December 2024